THE 5 GRACES

of life and leadership

Gary Burnison

CEO - Korn Ferry

Published by John Wiley & Sons, Inc., Hoboken, New Jersey.
Published simultaneously in Canada.

For general information on our other products and services or for technical support, please contact our Customer Care Department within the United States at (800) 762-2974, outside the United States at (317) 572-3993 or fax (317) 572-4002.

Wiley publishes in a variety of print and electronic formats and by print-on-demand. Some material included with standard print versions of this book may not be included in e-books or in print-on-demand. If this book refers to media such as a CD or DVD that is not included in the version you purchased, you may download this material at http://booksupport.wiley.com. For more information about Wiley products, visit www.wiley.com.

Library of Congress Cataloging-in-Publication Data

Names: Burnison, Gary, 1961- author. | John Wiley & Sons, publisher.
Title: The 5 graces of life and leadership / Gary Burnison.
Description: Hoboken, New Jersey : Wiley, [2022]
Identifiers: LCCN 2021047907 (print) | LCCN 2021047908 (ebook) | ISBN 9781119864042 (cloth) | ISBN 9781119864066 (adobe pdf) | ISBN 9781119864059 (epub)
Subjects: LCSH: Leadership--Study and teaching.
Classification: LCC HD57.7 .B865 2022 (print) | LCC HD57.7 (ebook) | DDC 658.4/092--dc23
LC record available at https://lccn.loc.gov/2021047907
LC ebook record available at https://lccn.loc.gov/2021047908

Cover Design: Korn Ferry - The LAB
Cover Photos by Dawid Zawiła, Matteo Vistocco, Amy Humphries,
        Bacila Vlad, Josue Escoto on Unsplash

SKY10029323_100621

Contents

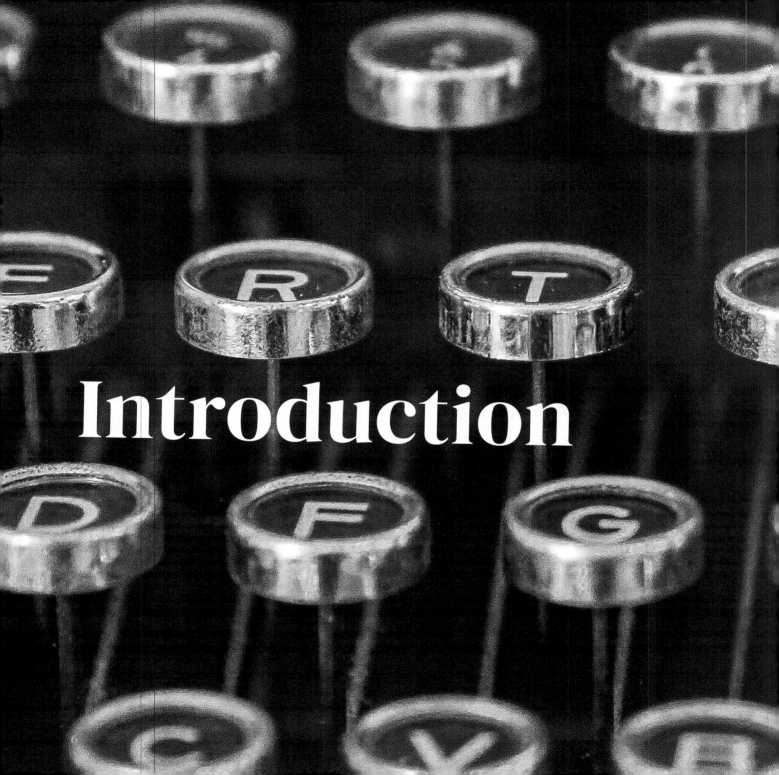

Introduction

Sitting on my desk is a pocket watch on a chain—
the one that has been passed down from my
grandfather to my father to me. My grandfather
carried it to work every day—first at the railroad
and later at a wheat mill. Its hands are frozen
at 7:39—whether a.m. or p.m., I'll never know.

Over the years, I've frequently held this watch
in my hand, a tangible connection to the past.
And it occurred to me: it will never tell time in
the present again. Sure, I could probably get it
fixed. But this heirloom is more poignant to me
as a reminder to savor the past, while not trying
to stay there. Time is the most precious
of all commodities—we can't make more of it.

Time has not stood still for any of us.

Today, we're seeing more change than we have
in the past 10 years. As the world tilts on its axis,
people are turning to leaders for help and hope,
direction and decision. After all, leadership
is inspiring others to believe and enabling
that belief to become reality.

And that takes grace.

Grace

I've had countless conversations about grace in the context of inspiring, motivating, and leading others. In each one, it struck me that—like truth, art, or love —grace is often hard to define. But we know it when we see it.

is.

Grace is a feeling

Grace is the

It moves us forward—elevating above any circumstance—and always along the high road. Grace is what makes us inherently human—the better self that shines a light for others.

gift of goodwill

Unearned and unmerited, grace
is present within each of us. It's as
old as human history—present in all
major cultures and religions. In Greek
mythology, the three daughters of Zeus
were known as the three Graces: Aglaea,
Euphrosyne, and Thalia. Their names—
translated as brightness, joyfulness,
and bloom (among others)—were the gifts
they gave to humanity. For us, the gift
is the goodwill of a human nature that
is predisposed to helping others.
We have joy when others are fulfilled.

Grace is an action

Images that come to mind may be
a dancer's poise, an athlete's fluid motion.
But true grace emerges through pressure
and sometimes under fire.

Grace is that voice of humility that
continually whispers, "It's not about you."

It calls us to accountability, responsibility,
and action. After all, the accountability we
want to see in others starts with each of us.

Grace is perspective

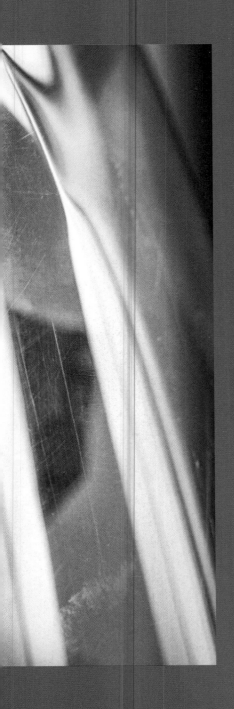

COVID-19 is not the first pandemic or crisis, nor will it be the last. This, too, will pass. We need to move beyond cause and effect because there are other forces at work—and this is where grace comes in. Grace is the goodness in all of us that comes out in times of pain and suffering.

Grace is the balance when emotions run high

Photo: Pedro Alves

It is tested at the extremes when we find it so hard to be graceful—in exuberance when we need to check our ego and in pessimism when we need to overcome fear. We are continually inspired by those who, despite their own upset, pain, and suffering, show only grace.

...ace is a virtue

It is evident the moment someone possessing it walks into a room. They are calm and confident, to the point of elegance. It's not only their assuring words that others need to hear, but also their cadence of how and when to deliver them. And even when the answer must be "no," grace conveys positivity that makes it feel like "yes." It's mindfulness, it's self-care, it's focusing on others. And, to be honest, it's all the things we didn't really talk about in the workplace before that have become more important than ever.

The five

graces

Leadership is the eighth wonder of the world. It is more seen and felt than defined and discussed. It's easy to intellectualize but elusive to actualize.

For nearly the past two years (and counting) I have been writing about leadership in "Special Editions"—sharing stories and thoughts about leading ourselves and others. These aren't just my thoughts, but are also the perspective of a firm with more than seven decades of world-class IP—that has conducted 70 million executive assessments and develops 1.2 million people a year.

In response to the Special Editions, I have been humbled by an outpouring of tens of thousands of emails, phone calls, conversations, and messages—thoughts, stories, and insights. Some brought a smile; others a tear. Some uplifted; some gave pause to reflect on another perspective. All spoke to the immutable power of hope—and the inherent grace of the human spirit.

This response is the inspiration for this book and
the Five Graces. Regardless of whether we lead a team
of five people or 50,000, or only ourselves, we need the
Five Graces. Each is an invaluable radically human trait
that in the aggregate literally compose the word grace:

Gratitude	**The attitude that lifts our hearts and elevates our spirits.**
Resilience	**What makes the impossible possible.**
Aspiration	**Knowing that we can make tomorrow different and better than today.**
Courage	**Not having "no fear," but rather to "know fear"—and move beyond it.**
Empathy	**Meeting others where they are to understand who they are.**

Grace is that voice
of humility that whispers,

"*It's not about you.*"

Grace reminds us of a paradox that is always true about leadership: it starts with the leader, but it is never about the leader.

Grace is that voice of humility that whispers, "It's not about you."

Here we find the softer side of leadership, far beyond any technical skillset that we have mastered in our careers. But make no mistake: each of the Five Graces contains hard truths that can make or break leadership—and there is nothing simple about them.

Grace keeps our focus on others. There is no leadership without followership. No leader wants to charge up the mountain only to discover halfway up that no one is following.

We recognize that leading is not about telling people what to do; rather, it's guiding them in what to think about. We know that while the leader sets the strategy, it takes others to execute that plan.

To have the grace to create this kind of leadership, we need to be radically human leaders with greater self-awareness and genuine connection to others. In today's new world, it's about establishing community so everyone can be part of something bigger than themselves.

It starts with **Gratitude**—the attitude that always determines our altitude. We need strength for the journey—that's where **Resilience** comes in. It propels us forward toward our **Aspirations** as we raise our sights on what we can become.

It also takes **Courage**—to look unblinkingly in the mirror and ask ourselves if we are truly committed to be the change we want to see in the world.

Last, but hardly least, we need **Empathy** to meet others where they are and to ensure that no one is left behind.

Leadership is always about transporting people.

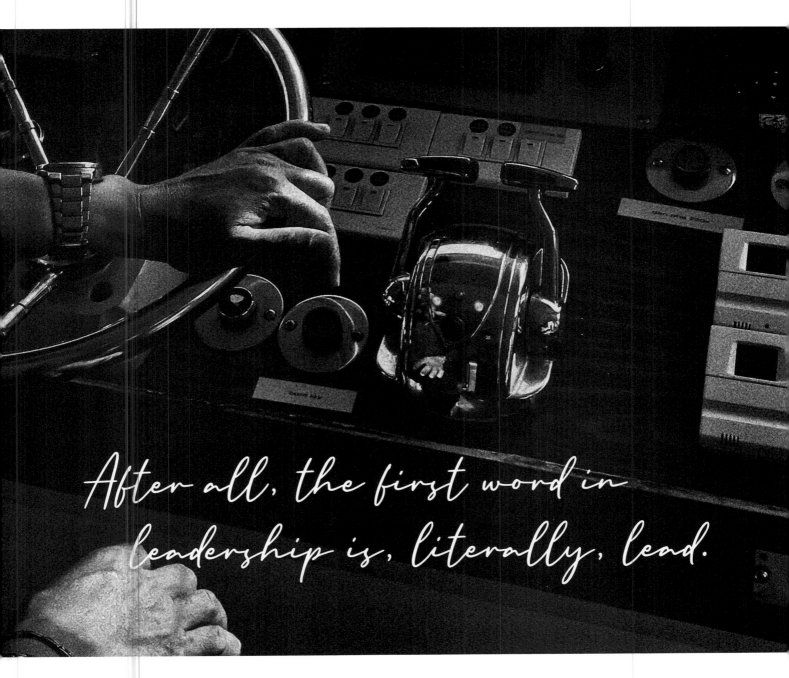

After all, the first word in leadership is, literally, lead.

Where grit

meets grace

When the going gets tough, and the way forward is shrouded in uncertainty, grit can push us through. It's the tenacious drive that makes us resilient against all odds. But grit alone cannot do the job—especially when leading others.

Grit reports to grace—the real sovereign. In the face of failure, grace assures us that we will not only be OK, but also actually get better. And, amid success, grace guards us against self-importance. What truly makes a difference is how we operate, the imprint we leave, and how we make others feel.

In other words, it is our grace.

Think about when the unexpected strikes. In every crisis, people look to others—who panicked, who had it together. And every time, they will train their eyes on the one person who exudes confidence that "everything will be OK."

Knowing that, we must ask ourselves: Are we the ones they turn to? No matter what happens, do we have the grit to be graceful?

Chapter 1
GRATITUDE

When people are told, "We couldn't have done this without you," the message delivered is, "You are loved."

Many years ago, early in my tenure as CEO, I went to New York to meet with a board member to go over the feedback of my 360-degree review. At the end of our three-hour conversation, that board member gave me invaluable advice that has guided me ever since:

"A leader's higher calling is to surround the organization with purpose. Your day job is to ensure that people feel better after every conversation with you than they did before."

I certainly don't always live up to that standard but showing appreciation starts with words that reflect sincere gratitude for others: Thank you. You're making a difference. You matter.

An attitude of gratitude starts with two small but extremely powerful words that translate in every language: thank you. It's a gift that goes both ways.

As we express our thanks, we are uplifted—often as much as the person being appreciated. Indeed, true gratitude is one of life's most precious treasures.

And for leaders, it is the saving grace.

The G in

Grace

Love and leadership aren't normally put together in the same sentence (for obvious reasons). But being radically human leaders begins with our hearts.

Face it: leaders need others—we all need others. Sincerely expressing our gratitude to others remains the most powerful way to change minds and win hearts.

That's why—and how—gratitude puts the G in grace. With gratitude, grace is not just the high road, it's the only road.

Years ago, if someone had asked me the traits of a CEO, I would have listed vision, a growth mindset, authenticity, confidence, courage ... I could see a place for humility. But vulnerability? That wouldn't have made it into my top 10.

But sometimes to show gratitude you must be vulnerable. Vulnerability is a real strength for connecting with others—authentically and with empathy. Sure, we need to use our brains—with ideas, strategies, and analytics that are increasingly the table stakes of leadership. And we need guts—better known as courage—to make sure that we're aligned with our values. But the heart matters most.

Leading

We never really get out of the sixth grade. Think about it—we're all still motivated by the same desires that used to rule the playground: we want to be liked, to be accepted, to get picked for the team, to be popular.

We all want to be seen—in every aspect of our lives. We hunger for affirmation. We want to know that we matter—we make a difference to others. As we acknowledge this hunger within ourselves, we know how important it is for others to feel our gratitude for who they are and all that they do.

For most people, it comes down to two motivators: for love or for money. Money can rent loyalty, but it can't buy it. Love wins out every time. People want to be loved and they want to belong—and the most potent rewards address both of those desires.

Affirming others, however, is more than the generic "good job" or even "I'm proud of you." Affirmation is the heartfelt "I believe in you"—and it expresses our gratitude in a way that empowers others. As a member of our board, who mentored me in my early days as a CEO, once told me: "I don't just want you to be successful—I am going to ensure that you are successful." In those words, he told me he was invested in me.

We can never say "I believe in you" too often. I see you. I value you. You matter. You make a difference…. When people are told "We couldn't have done this without you," the message delivered is, "You are loved."

with heart

Affirmation is the heartfelt "I believe in you"—and it expresses our gratitude in a way that empowers others.

The gift of gratitude

Over the years, I've had the privilege of working with colleagues who readily expressed their genuine respect, appreciation, and love for others. I'll never forget how one of our leaders, the late Bob McNabb, signed off every conversation with almost everyone he knew: "Love you, babe." That was Bob!

Another colleague often ends his conversations with "Love home." It's his unique shorthand for good wishes to the person and their family or loved ones. When I asked my colleague about his tagline, he replied, "It's endemic to my soul. It feels more natural to say, 'Love home,' instead of just 'good-bye.'"

Each time we express our appreciation, we uplift others. That's the joy of being the giver—whether of inspiring words, thoughtful support, or a small token of thanks. Being the recipient, however, can be both humbling and moving, as I experienced a few years ago.

A colleague and I were traveling together, and as we passed through a very remote airport, we passed a boot shop. In the window was a pair of bright red cowboy boots.

"Those are the bomb," I said, half joking.

Imagine my surprise on the plane when my colleague, brimming with a wide smile, brought out a box—yep, the cowboy boots. The next day, as I got ready for a speech before hundreds of business leaders and then a meeting with a billionaire (who, at the time, was the world's wealthiest person), I decided to wear those boots. Not my usual business attire, but I knew my friend and colleague would be so pleased. After all, his gift of the boots was a tangible expression of appreciation to me. And by wearing the boots to a very important meeting, I gave him the gift of my sincerest gratitude.

When we walked into the billionaire's office, there were stacks of papers and books everywhere. Sitting at his desk, going over a thick report, our host was clearly distracted and did not seem to pay much attention to us as we sat down. Then, at the end of our two-hour meeting, he gave me a sly smile and said, "So, where's the horse?"

We all laughed. What was truly amazing, though, was that this billionaire, who appeared unaware of anything except the papers in front of his nose, had noticed. Nothing was beyond his line of sight. And my colleague's smile made it all worthwhile.

The gift we never return

We've all had this experience: giving someone a gift and waiting for the wrapping paper to be removed and the box opened. Nervous and a little uncertain, and even to hedge our bets, we whisper when no one's listening, "There's a gift receipt at the bottom if you want to take it back."

Not so with the gift of pure, unadulterated appreciation. There are no receipts, no strings attached. This is not layaway for some future obligation. It's all gratitude. People should not need to read the tea leaves in an email or a text—anxiously interpreting the emoji or discerning the meaning of a period after "thank you" instead of an exclamation point. When we are truly thankful, there should be no doubt about it. Others can feel it, in our words and in our actions. This gift never gets returned.

The power of one

On my computer is a Post-It note—
the stickiness long worn off and now
fastened with a piece of tape. On it is
a quotation from Edward Everett Hale,
a nineteenth-century social reformer
and minister, that was shared with me
by an executive more than a year ago:

I am only one; but still I am one. I cannot do everything; but still I can do something; and because I cannot do everything, I will not refuse to do the something that I can do.

These words have taken on so much meaning about the importance of one. No matter how powerless we may feel, no matter how big the problems in the world, we can still do that "something" that we all can do. We can show genuine caring and gratitude.

Did anyone tell great you are today?

An executive shared a story with me of her 92-year-old grandfather who made it a habit to deliver a heartfelt message to everyone who made a difference in his life —be they family members, friends, or someone who served him at the local diner:

"Did anyone tell you how great you are today?"

"I've heard this line thousands of times," the executive told me. "Yet it still snaps me out of whatever mindset I am in and humbles me into a simpler state of mind— of being loved and seen."

It's the secret to sustainable success: when people are recognized, they're happy; and when they're happy, they're motivated. And if they're motivated, they're more likely to outperform. Our gratitude lifts others up. Gratitude makes all the difference.

you how

„

Photo: Boris Thaser

Gratitude makes

all

the difference.

There's always time for gratitude

"How is everyone holding up?"
a colleague in Brazil was asked
during a particularly intense time.

He responded philosophically and pivoted
the conversation to gratitude, which as
he explained has deep meaning in Latin
American culture. Instead of thinking
about what is missing, instead of voicing
regrets or dissatisfaction, there is always
time to be grateful for what we have.

When gratitude goes AWOL

People everywhere hunger to be seen, to feel valued. They want to be noticed and acknowledged.

But, if we're honest, the challenge for some leaders is the first big disconnect—the broken bridge between knowing and doing.

It's not that managers and bosses don't care—or that they're not nice people. All too often, though, the pace of play and the volume of activity get in the way. And that's true at every level and in every position.

Not showing gratitude by recognizing, rewarding, and celebrating others carries a high cost—namely, weaker bonds within a listless, lifeless organization. That's the second big disconnect —and everyone suffers.

It's a fact of life: when an emotional connection is missing, people may begin to deliver only what needs to get done but may not tap any discretionary energy at their disposal. Unfortunately, that makes it easier for them to walk out the door.

For many people these days, the connective tissue is gone —and they want a fresh start. They want to understand the team they're playing for—what's the vision? What do the values mean for them? It all comes down to the people you work with, the boss you report to, and how engaged and inspired you feel.

A helping hand

At the risk of oversimplification, it comes down to gratitude. People want to feel gratified by their work—and that others notice and are grateful for them.

I learned that lesson in a most unexpected place.

I was sitting on a curb along a highway in Oklahoma. It was one of just a few trips I'd taken in almost a year and a half, and I was driving a rental car along an unfamiliar road. I wasn't quite sure where I was, cell phone reception was sketchy, and I couldn't figure out which button did what. So, with a conference call coming up, I pulled over to the shoulder and found a place where the signal was strong and my mind was clear.

That's when another vehicle pulled off the pavement and rolled to a stop a few feet from where I sat.

"Do you need help?" the driver and a passenger asked. "Do you know where you're going?"

With sincere thanks, I assured them I was fine.

The whole interaction took only a few minutes, but it was so welcome and refreshing— connecting with strangers who extended a helping hand. And I was grateful.

Catch people doing things right

What gets measured doesn't just get done, as the well-known saying goes. It also must get celebrated—all along the way! It used to be that everyone waited until the big milestone was reached. When asked, "Now that you've won [fill in the blank], what are you going to do?" The answer was, "We're going to Disneyland!"

That's great, but radically human leaders don't hold off celebrating until some end point. Rather, they find reasons to celebrate the journey. When we acknowledge and celebrate how far we've come, we are even more inspired about what we can become. In the words of leadership guru Ken Blanchard, "Catch people doing things right."

It's up to the leader to create a culture of recognition and celebration.

Listening to that voice

Making a list of priorities is easy—to do, not do, decide, delegate. That's table stakes. But what about those things we willfully and intentionally put aside because they take too much time and effort? Or perhaps they make us appear weak and vulnerable.

We need to ask ourselves the hardest questions—probing what we intuitively know we should be doing, but far too often we fail and forget:

Do I spend the time to make sure someone feels better after an interaction with me versus how they felt before —and do I really care?

Do I just assume people know I appreciate them, or do I actually take the time to say, "Thank you"?

Is there daylight between my words and my actions?

How do I provide meaning to others?

Our gratitude is indeed our team's altitude.

Believe it. Say it. Mean it. Act it.

Chapter 2

RESILIENCE

Fatigue casts a long shadow.

It can only be dispelled by the light of resilience.

We've all heard the "stories behind the stories"—of what people have been through and experienced in life. As much as we might like to wish some of it away, we really have no other choice than to make a path forward.

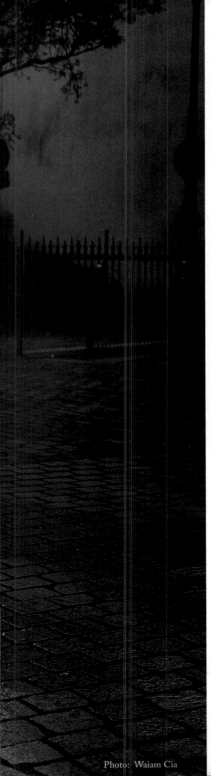

When I was about 15 years old, I needed surgery on my foot because of a basketball injury. It was a minor procedure with a local anesthetic. Afterwards I felt fine—my foot was still numb. My dad drove me, and on the way home we stopped at the grocery store. Since I had this big "boot" on, I stayed in the car.

I waited and waited, but still my dad didn't come out of the store. I began to wonder what was keeping him. When an ambulance pulled up, I had a weird intuition that sent me hobbling inside. There was Dad, lying unconscious on that grocery store floor with a pool of blood next to his head.

I rode with him in the ambulance to the hospital, where I was told that he'd had a heart attack. By the time he was fully conscious and out of danger, it was nearly midnight. Since I didn't have any money, I had no choice but to walk home—it was probably four or five miles.

The anesthetic had worn off and the pain was nearly unbearable. But with every step, I told myself to keep moving— one foot ahead of the other.

That day, I learned an invaluable lesson. Paraphrasing the words of Spanish poet Antonio Machado, we make our path as we walk it.

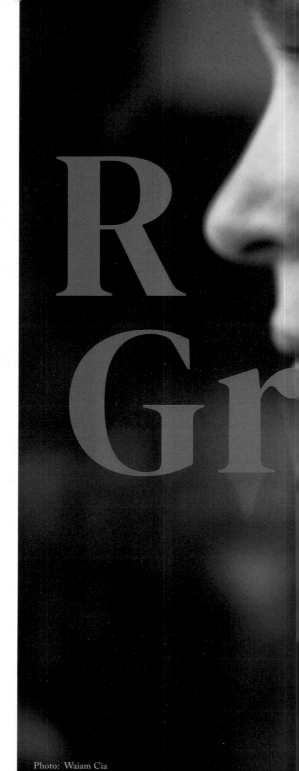

The R in Gr

Resilience propels us forward—no matter what.

And that's why resilience puts the R in grace. It is the energy recharge that makes the impossible possible.

ace

When the proverbial going gets tough, we can procrastinate, pause, or push forward. To keep moving, we must harness the immutable power of *resilience.*

The mightiness of resilience

The occasion was a regular meeting of our leadership team—and I decided to start it differently. I asked each of our leaders, from around the globe, what they thought were the most important themes of the day. Their answers ranged from the clout of connectedness to practicing patience.

Overall, a few themes emerged: Empathy for others. The fragility of the world. The empowerment of stillness. The power of all.

But the one we kept coming back to was the mightiness of resilience. Always and everywhere, it is the ultimate renewable energy source for leaders and their teams.

74

When we hit that wall

The concert hall was packed. I had a good seat with a clear view of the stage as the pianist—the star of the show—began to play flawlessly. Then, halfway through Rachmaninoff's Third Piano Concerto, he suddenly stopped.

His hands froze on the keys, and he bowed his head. He turned to us and said, "I don't want to play in public anymore." This world-renowned performer had simply hit the wall. Whatever the reason, he could not play one … more … note.

Shining our light of resilience takes energy.

There are times in life when we know that what we're facing won't be a sprint. And it may not even be a marathon. Sometimes we find ourselves in the midst of an Ironman triathlon —a 2.4-mile swim, a 112-mile bicycle ride, followed by a 26.2-mile marathon— all raced in that order for safety and performance.

When we step across the finish line, it doesn't matter how long it takes to get there—how fast or slow we run. Getting to that point is everything.

And just like a runner after a marathon, we cannot just sit down. We have to stay in motion, and then it's time to stretch—to celebrate, recalibrate, rejuvenate. We pause in order to savor just how far we've come—staying flexible, nimble, and agile—while building our strength so we have the resilience for the next race.

Hope is resilience

Many of us have heard stories from our parents, grandparents, and other relatives about what it was like to be children during the Great Depression and then young adults during World War II, which meant everything from military service to rationing at home.

The impact of these stories lives on, reminding us that no matter what challenges we face, there is always a way.

Indeed, over the millennia, humans have faced countless catastrophes—and with far less science and technology than we have today. Our hope is always in the resilience of the human spirit.

Our leap of faith

When we were kids, hot summer weekends usually meant one thing—going to the local swimming pool. Sitting on the edge of that pool, we'd dangle our toes in the water and look up at the high dive. It didn't seem *that* tall. Then we started climbing the ladder, one rung at a time.

When we reached the fifth rung, with what seemed like a hundred more ahead of us, beads of sweat were rolling down our faces. The only thing that kept us going was the fear of being teased by the other kids if we suddenly reversed course and climbed back down. But that was exactly what we wanted to do.

Finally, we reached the top. Staring down the length of that diving board, we felt as if we were walking the plank.

Then, looking down at our toes as we tried to grip the board, we saw something in our peripheral vision—our friends, bobbing in the water. Just moments before, they had taken the plunge.

Their reality became our resilience.

That's when we heard their encouraging words: "You can do this!" In an instant, perspective shifted—and off we went.

In the same way, to build our resilience today, we can't go it alone. We need good coaching—the guiding hand, the gentle nudge. It's caring combined with directness. Coaches are the voice of assurance and reason.

Our support comes from "capital C coaches" who have formal training, certification, and experience to help others, as well as informal "lowercase C coaches" who listen and encourage—and that means us. People always look to leaders, not only for advice and counsel, but also for role modeling being resilient—and taking that leap of faith.

A good coach can
be that still, small
voice that tells us,

" Don't give up!"

83

Failing to fail

Nothing builds resilience quite like failure.

That's important to keep in mind these days as leaders everywhere ponder the question: How can we keep people feeling motivated and empowered?

My answer, surprisingly perhaps, starts with failure.

Think about it. If people are afraid to fail—if there are punishments or if rewards are withheld because of failure—then people won't feel empowered to take chances. More than that, they'll never build the muscles that will help them get up and start again.

The most important aspect of failure is not the moment of defeat or loss. It's what we do in the moment after that. It's never about the fall—it's about getting back up. It's not about the failure—it's about the learning.

Failure is usually temporary; it passes like a storm. So why would we let it paralyze us? What are we really afraid of? Is it that we can't stand the possibility of failing? The bigger question to ask is, What greater accomplishment or goal could we achieve if we never gave into our fears? What might others become if failure became part of our culture?

Truly, the only real failure will be failing to fail.

When people know it's safe to fail, they'll become much more resilient.

Getting back on that bike

A colleague shared this story from the earliest days of his career, when he had an on-campus interview with a large accounting firm. As he was getting dressed, he realized his suit was still in his car. Barefoot, wearing a dress shirt and shorts, he went outside—without any of his keys. Suddenly, he was locked out, with no suit, no keys, no access to his apartment, no way to get into his car—and the interview was fast approaching.

Desperate, he stopped a guy on the street he didn't know who was about his size and asked to borrow a suit, tie, belt, and shoes. To top it off, he borrowed the guy's bicycle, which he rode four miles to the interview. When he showed up late, the interviewer was not amused.

So, my colleague grasped the only chance he saw to turn the situation around. "A funny thing happened on the way to this interview…." By the end of the story, the interviewer was laughing and said, "Anybody who could show that much creativity and resilience is exactly the type of employee we're looking for."

Coming

out of the fog

When we're in the thick of it—the turbulence, the storm—clouds of uncertainty and ambiguity shade the horizon. We can easily get lost as our perceptions are skewed.

But the horizon is always ahead. Our only choice is embracing that the unexpected is to be expected.

The challenge is that it's not always easy to see. Based on assessments of millions of executives, we've found that 90% of the problems they face are ambiguous. With greater responsibility comes even more ambiguity in all its forms: uncertainty, obscurity, vagueness, doubt, and enigma.

Instead of running from ambiguity—avoiding the illusion—we need to embrace it.

Rowing in unison

It's been said that the strength of a team is each individual member—and the strength of each individual member is the team. Resilience builds in both directions.

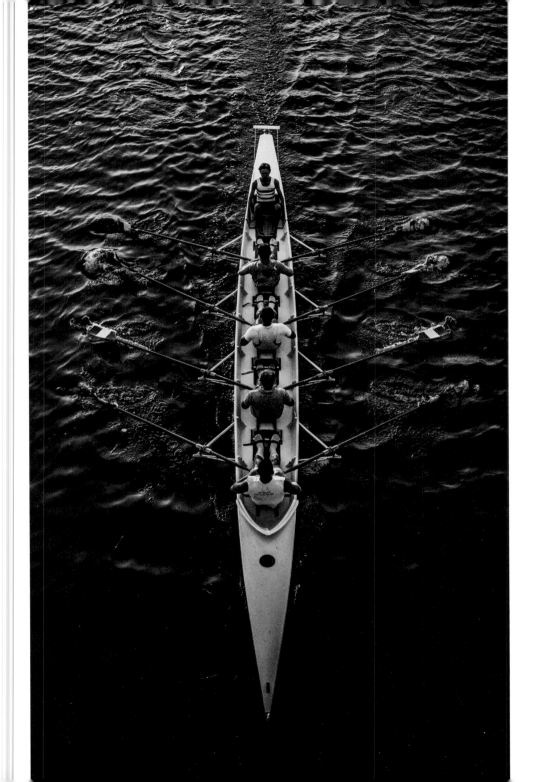

Our resilience not only energizes us; it also empowers others.

The essence of any leadership journey is transporting people from one place to another—inspiring them to believe in what they can achieve. An analogy I've used to illustrate this is to imagine leading thousands of people from diverse backgrounds, countries, experiences, and perspectives on a cross-country trip— New York to Los Angeles—by foot.

Not everyone is in the same place. Some people are bringing burdens— losses, weariness, loneliness. At times, it may seem like heresy to ask them to take one more step, to do one more thing. Others, though, long to sprint ahead—they can't wait to get moving.

Along the way, leaders are "shepherds"— sometimes in front, sometimes behind, but always beside others. It's never about power—but rather **empower**.

Our metamorphosis

Metamorphosis is not a choice —it's a reality.

This goes way beyond merely rebirth or cyclical regeneration like the cicadas that leave their subterranean world every 17 years to spend a few noisy weeks above ground. Trillions of them emerge en masse to ensure that enough survive to procreate, instead of becoming nature's high-protein snack.

But even after 17 years, a cicada is still a cicada—unchanged. Not so with the butterfly, which undergoes one of the most dramatic metamorphoses in nature. It begins life crawling and ends up soaring.

I witnessed this a few years ago, during a time of pure powerlessness against a wave of devastation that had come out of nowhere and mushroomed into a life-threatening risk. Wildfires in California were destroying millions of acres and countless homes and cost many lives. One fire was perilously close to where I live, impacting thousands of people. Houses in our neighborhood were burned to the ground, although several (including ours) were spared by a shift in the wind.

But that was not the end of the story.

Heavy rains followed the wildfires. Slowly, life returned. Nature, ever resilient, greened the canyons and flowers began to bloom where, not long before, there had been only charred earth. Then one day, as I drove to the beach, millions of butterflies filled the air. I couldn't believe what I was seeing at first—it didn't seem real. I slowed the car and watched as they sailed over the windshield, never striking it.

It was a sea of butterflies, the ultimate symbol of metamorphosis.

Just like those butterflies, we can burst out of our cocoons, transmuting loss into learning.

The new world belongs to the most resilient.

Where resilience meets reality

I once started a leadership meeting by showing a picture and asking people what they saw. Most people, with a bias toward optimism, focused on the foreground where a young girl was picking flowers. A smaller number said their focus was drawn to the dilapidated buildings in the background. Only 2 out of 17 said they focused on both.

That's what I was driving at: while there was hope and optimism (the flowers), pessimism and reality tell us there will always be risks and challenges to overcome (the decayed buildings).

Our biggest blind spot is getting stuck in the past, defaulting to the way things used to be. With agility and resolve, we rise to meet whatever reality demands of us.

Look up, look out, leap forward. No matter the obstacles we face or the challenges ahead, there's always a way forward. We do, indeed, make our path as we walk it.

Chapter 3

ASPIRATION

Aspiration is the knowledge that we can make tomorrow

different and better

than today.

We felt like we could reach out and touch the stars.

A few years ago, my family and I went stargazing in a remote location. Without city lights to obscure our view, every tiny dot of brilliance shone crystal clear. As we looked through the telescope, we were awestruck by the countless stars and swirls of the Milky Way. In that moment, we felt connected to something bigger than ourselves.

Today, we all need this same cosmic shift in perspective. When we look through the eyepiece of a telescope, what is distant suddenly zooms closer. But if we look through the wrong end of the telescope, things shrink away from us.

We need to ask ourselves: Which end of the telescope are we looking through?

Even when things seem so far away, they are much closer than they appear. When we clearly see just how far we've come, we appreciate more fully just how capable we've become.

And it's not just about us.

As we raise our sights, we elevate others, as well. Their aspirations become our

inspiration.

The A
n Grace

Desire. Longing. Yearning. Wish. . Each of these terms help define ion—yet it is bigger than all of them. tion is not just a momentary want— ing to attain in the moment. It is n—a goal. It is more than what we achieve—it embodies what t to become.

why aspiration is the A in grace

Aspiration sets our sights on the future. When others only see clouds, as leaders we must show them that it's possible to punch a hole right through—

to the blue sky above.

What lens are we looking through?

Mindset is a conscious choice—one we make every minute of every day. We need to ask ourselves: What lens are we looking through? Do we resist change? Or do we embrace it as a chance to expand our perspectives and seek out opportunities to meet new people, learn new things, and have new experiences?

Paraphrased slightly, Aldous Huxley, the philosopher and author, observed: "Experience is not what happens to you; it is what you do with what happens to you."

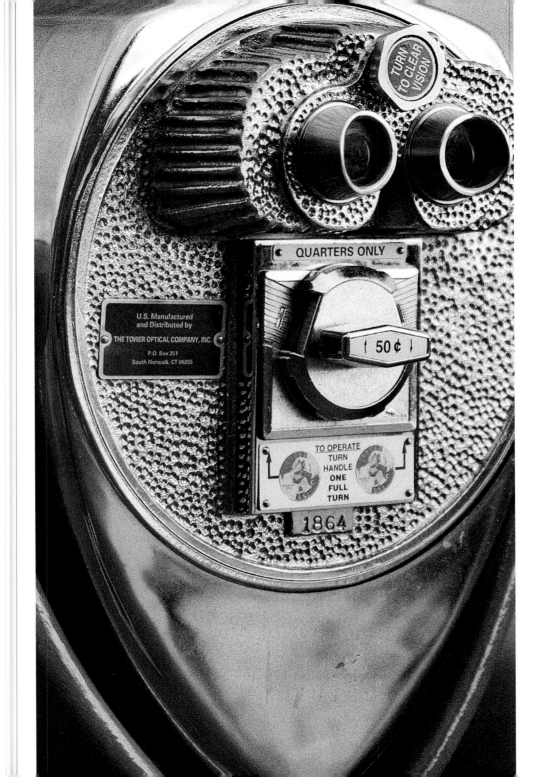

The open road

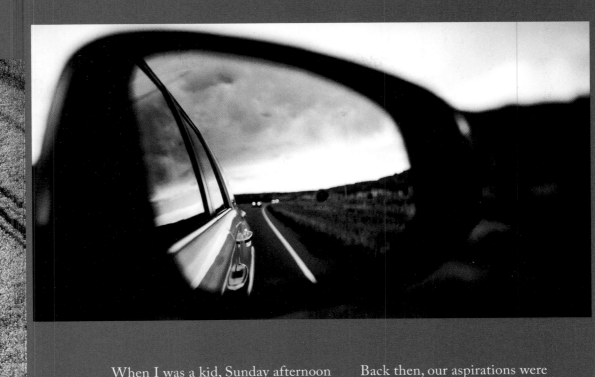

When I was a kid, Sunday afternoon drives were a big deal—starting the moment somebody jangled the car keys and said, "Let's go for a ride."

I can remember sitting in the back seat of our old car—the windows rolled down, the radio up, and the breeze in our faces. We didn't live in a big town—it took less than 10 minutes to drive from one end to the other. Once we crossed the city line, though, there was nothing but central Kansas farm fields and open road.

Back then, our aspirations were nothing more than just going— for miles and miles—and only for the pure pleasure of the experience.

It was like Alice in Wonderland asking the Cheshire Cat for directions—but not really caring about where she gets to. And so, as the Cheshire Cat observes, "Then it doesn't matter which way you go."

It was all about being in motion— and sometimes, that's enough.

Fast-forward to another Sunday drive, when I was an adult, visiting in the Midwest. "I want to show you something," a friend of mine told me. And so we started out with a very specific purpose, destination, and outcome in mind.

Our objective: the Hutchinson salt mines, now part museum. As a young boy, I had been given salt rocks (I can remember licking them to taste the saltiness) but hadn't thought much about where they'd come from. And even if someone had told me, I couldn't have imagined it—not until I saw it with my own eyes.

My friend and I stood in a cavernous mine—some 650 feet underground and a constant 68 degrees. The Hutchinson Salt Company mine covers 980 acres, and the network of tunnels measures 150 miles. Stored in a secure area of the mine—safe from floods, fires, and tornadoes—are priceless collections, from the original footage of Hollywood classics to valuable documents from all 50 states and foreign countries.

Until that moment, I never knew what had existed all along—right below my feet. And all it took was someone to show me.

Just like when we took those Sunday afternoon drives, we all need to ask ourselves:

Where will our aspirations take us next?

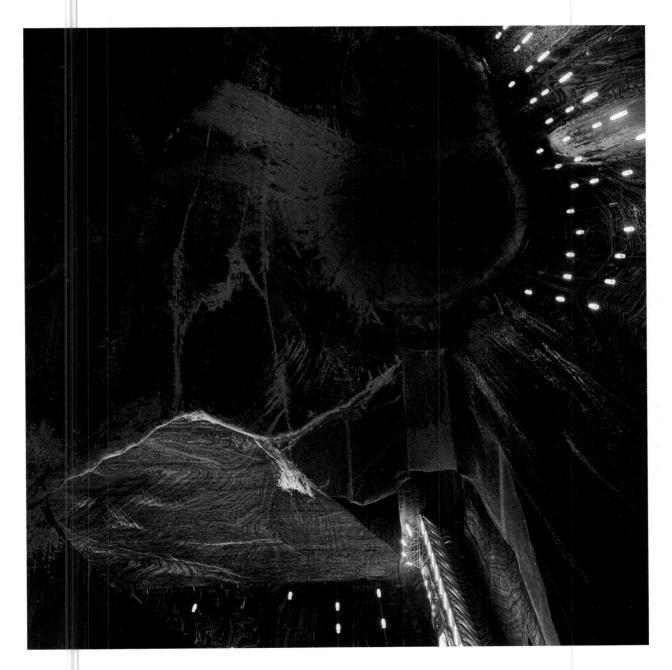

Keeping it real

Too much of a good thing is still too much—even when it's hope and aspiration. It comes down to balance, where hope meets reality—and it must be constantly recalibrated. That starts at the top.

It's the role of the leader to convey meaning, a shared way of understanding—with realism on one side and reassurance on the other, and reward and risk in between. It's a Monte Carlo simulation in action as we anticipate what lies ahead by accurately perceiving today's reality. But when we connect with people, it's important to be realistically optimistic.

Yet there are people who struggle with the opposite scenario. They're immersed in pessimistic reality, while hope remains elusive.

We need to remember —while reality keeps us grounded, hope will always inspire.

Our Ode
to Joy

As a college student, I could not have imagined two more different musical experiences. First, I'd scraped together the money to hear Queen at the Forum. Then, a month later, a friend was given tickets to hear the Los Angeles Philharmonic perform Beethoven's Ninth Symphony at the Hollywood Bowl, and I was dragged along.

Sitting there, staring at the program, two thoughts went through my mind: What was I doing here, and how long was this going to last? My biggest desire was to get out of there as fast as possible.

When the Philharmonic launched into the Ninth Symphony's first movement, I naively stifled a groan—it sounded like a musical anesthetic. Then, before I was even aware, a repeating melody hooked me. By the fourth and final movement—Beethoven's famous "Ode to Joy"—that soaring, triumphant music shook the Hollywood Bowl to its foundation. Individually, people were moved, but the collective uplift that swept through that amphitheater was palpable.

I remember that shared experience to this day, and it can be described only by one word—joy.

When Beethoven wrote his Ninth Symphony, between 1822 and 1824, he had lost his hearing—but not his passion. Inspired by the ideals of his age—of enlightenment and unity—Beethoven aspired to set Friedrich Schiller's poem "Ode to Joy" to music. He became the first major composer to create a choral symphony combining instruments and voices. It was a shared experience that needed to be created, heard, seen, and felt. Today, it is regarded as Beethoven's greatest work.

Over the centuries, "Ode to Joy" has become a tribute of hope and unity. It has marked Olympic Games and the fall of the Berlin Wall and was adopted as the anthem of the European Union.

Now, as we set our sights on the future, we need to ask ourselves:

"What is our Ode to Joy?"

longing to belong

Merely fitting in is superficial—
like slipping into a room unnoticed.
The power of belonging is bigger.
Belonging taps into our deepest,
fundamental longing to connect
to something bigger than ourselves.
We want to be loved, to know
that what we do matters.
We want to be seen and heard.

Creating a sense of community
and unity is more important than
ever. We need to articulate just
how much every person matters
because what the organization
wants is not motivation enough.

It's all about what individuals
aspire to—and helping to make
those dreams come true.

Aspiring to inspire

In bull markets, people look to the leader for validation. In bear markets, they look to the leader for reassurance. It's hope and grace, combined.

As leaders, it's not just what we say that gives others the hope, assurance, and belief they need. It's how we say it—our tone, energy, and attitude. After all, we're not just messengers— we *are* the message.

But people's attention must be earned, not merely taken for granted. The best way to do that is by telling a story—and everyone has one. Connective and cathartic, our stories tell of our joy and suffering, triumph and tragedy—defining who we are, and who we're becoming.

Of course, not everyone can give a spontaneous TED Talk or hold an audience spellbound. Nor do we have to. We just need to be ourselves— vulnerable and authentic.

Indeed, the more we reveal about ourselves, the more others will share of themselves. I'll never forget the day a colleague reached out with a message that was humbling in its honesty and vulnerability: "I wanted to share my story, which I have never shared with anyone in the corporate world before...."

There are personal stories— raw and filled with emotion. There are stories of people finally feeling free to be who they truly are. There are shared stories of hardship and humble beginnings—now told with pride, not shame. Never about the polish and the presentation, these storytellers bare their souls to punctuate the reality they lived.

The best stories unify us through common experiences, while also celebrating the differences that broaden our thinking.

They inspire
to aspire.

Bringing others ashore

It's true that leaders are in the "what," "how," and "when" business. But ultimately, we all must be in the "opportunity" business—because exceeding potential is not just about each of us, it's about all of us.

A fable, which was shared with me by a colleague, captures this perfectly. A ship out in the middle of the ocean was rocked by a fierce storm. Everyone had to abandon ship. After countless days in a small life raft, the captain finally stood on the beach of a deserted island, surrounded by 10 other wet, cold, and scared people.

Instinctively, the captain reassured the others that they would be rescued. In the meantime, the priorities were shelter, fire, and food. People worked together in small groups— and they began to believe.

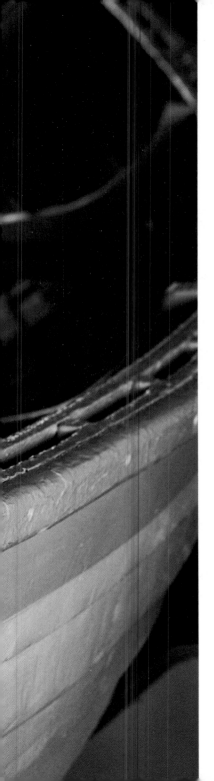

The captain climbed a hill above the beach to search the horizon for signs of a rescuer. Instead, the captain saw at least 10 more life rafts being carried toward the island by the tide. "We're going to have company," the captain called out to the others. "Soon, there will be 100 or so people on this beach—and they need our help."

"Lucky for them, you're here to take charge," someone called out from the group, and many others nodded.

"No," said the captain. "That's not going to work. There will be too many for one person to lead directly. I need each of you to meet one life raft and help those people for the next few days until we get rescued."

The group didn't look happy. "How will we do that?" they asked.

"The same way I did," the captain said. "It's not that difficult—reassure them about their future, help them understand what needs to be done now, and be clear about their accountability within their capabilities."

"So, what will you be doing?" another person asked.

The captain explained: "It's my job to help each of you become the leader that your team needs."

Always and everywhere, people are in search of hope, help, and heroes. We must each rise up and

bring them ashore.

The ABCs of leadership

Just as in the fable, we need the ABCs of leadership: accountability, belief, and capability.

The **accountability** we wish to see in others starts with each of us. In other words, we must first be accountable to ourselves for our own behaviors. Believe it, say it, mean it, act it!

The **belief** that we can make a difference—that change is possible—puts us into action. But if we don't believe, we won't achieve.

Capability is a broad brush: listening, connecting, inspiring, giving and getting honest feedback, expanding networks, exploring with others, and constantly looking for opportunities to learn. It's all about allowing belief and accountability to shine through our actions.

As good as our last promise

First, we must believe. After all, leadership is inspiring others to believe and enabling that belief to become reality.

Then we must encourage trust. In fact, we can think of belief and trust as forming two lanes of the highway.

For others to trust us, we must say what we mean and do what we say. There can be no daylight between the two.

We're only as good as our last promise kept.

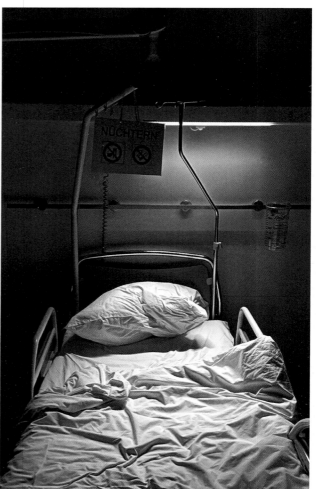

Hope never dies

I'll never forget the day I took my dog on a long walk, just to clear my head. I came upon a stretch of pavement that literally stopped me in my tracks. Scrawled in chalk, in a child's handwriting, were the words: "Everything will be OK."

Immediately, I was yanked back to years earlier when my son, Jack, then five years old, was in a sterile white pre-op room at a hospital getting ready to undergo surgery. We had all been calm the night before, but after getting up at the crack of dawn, the gravity of it hit when the nurse came in to put a needle in Jack's arm.

His eyes wide, Jack turned to me and asked, "Daddy, will everything be OK?"

Every parent throughout time has surely been asked this question, but for me that was the first time. Startled by the sheer fear I felt inside, I forced confidence into my voice. "Yes," I told him. "It's going to be OK."

Many years later, our roles were reversed. I was in a hospital bed, having herniated a disk in my back for the third time. As I was ready to go into surgery, Jack squeezed my arm and said those same words to me: "Dad, everything is going to be OK."

Hope camouflages fear and catalyzes belief. Our thoughts turn away from the negative and rush toward the positive. And then we know with absolute certainty: tomorrow will be different and better than today.

We see what others cannot perceive. We paint a picture of what they cannot yet envision. Like the brushstrokes on canvas—or the innocence of a child's drawing on pavement—these images and messages raise hope, instill confidence, and embolden our aspirations.

Tomorrow will
be different and
better than today.

Chapter 4
COURAGE

Courage is not "no fear" but rather to

" **know fear** "

I will never forget the first time
I got caught in an ocean riptide.

I was young, and in my panic, my first instinct was to swim toward shore as fast and as hard as I could. But I never got anywhere. Instead, I sank, lower and lower.

Fortunately, an older teenager was out there with me. He grabbed my shoulder and yelled, "You need to swim the other way!"

By the time I finally reached the beach, I was so exhausted I fell to my knees, completely spent. But I learned an invaluable lesson: instead of fighting the current, I had to go with it.

That same lesson applies whenever we face ambiguity and anxiety. Admittedly, those moments can be very hard. Anxiety is energy without a goal.

But they are opportunities to learn—and coach others—in becoming more comfortable with being uncomfortable. The first step is to have the courage to pause—zoom out and tap Google Earth to gain a broader perspective to understand the circumstances. Context can be liberating! Then, with courage comes clarity and acceptance.

The Cin

Grace

Courage is the C in grace—and for good reason.

During times of rapid change, being "up in the air" can feel uncomfortable. Even when we look ahead with optimism, the reality is we're not quite there yet. We're in transition—moving from one place (physical, mental, or emotional) to the next.

We're like trapeze artists. When we're flying through the air, we can't make the next trapeze appear automatically—we have to wait for it. Then, as it approaches, we have to let go of the old trapeze so we can reach for the new one.

In that moment—completely ungrounded—we need the courage to pause so we can bring ourselves closer to whatever comes next.

Pushing pause

It sounds paradoxical, but even
though leaders must have the confidence
to act quickly, they can't just flip
a switch. They need to move at a
pace the organization can absorb.

This does not mean slowing down.
But it does mean we need to pause
occasionally so we can continually and
accurately assess today's ever-changing
reality. Then, after that brief pause, we
will have greater understanding that helps
us anticipate scenarios of what lies ahead.

Knowing

fear

On the wall behind my desk at home is a beautiful framed print—black brushstrokes against an off-white background— a gift given to me a few years ago by colleagues in China. The translation, on a brass plaque at the bottom, reads:

"The Courageous have no Fear – Confucius (551 B.C.)."

It is part of a longer quote that has been translated as: "the humane do not worry; the wise are not perplexed; the courageous have no fear." It is an expression of an ideal—an extraordinarily high bar. I view the words not only as solace, but also as encouragement.

We need guts, better known as courage, to be authentic and aligned with our values. With a strong sense of purpose, we can say and do what needs to get said and done without fear—especially of failure.

Having no fear of failure does not imply that leaders have never failed or that they will not fail in the future. It does not equate to brashness or bravado. If anything, it is the opposite. No matter what materializes—whether success or failure—it's courage that counts.

It's true of every great leader: they exhibit tremendous courage around the possibility— and even the inevitability at times—of failure. They recognize that failure is never fatal—provided that learning occurs.

Courage:

Acknowledging what you don't know

At age 13, I wasn't really ready for a driving lesson, and I couldn't get a learner's permit for another year. But my dad decided to take me to the cemetery parking lot to practice a little. His hand was on mine as he guided me through the "three on the tree" pattern of the shifter on the steering column.

He also grabbed the steering wheel a couple of times—like when I rounded a corner a little too sharply, jumped a curb, and nearly clipped a tombstone.

With time and practice, I began to get the hang of that three-speed transmission. I can still remember the H pattern—first gear, second gear, third gear, reverse, with neutral in between.

The first time
any of us do
anything,
more often
than not
someone
shows us
how, instead
of us trying
to do it all on
our own.

Knowledge is what we know.

Courage is
acknowledging
what we
don't know.

As we process what we've learned we
can apply those lessons going forward
as we face new and first-time challenges.
In other words, we develop learning
agility—or, as I call it, knowing what
to do when you don't know what to do.
And it's the number-one predictor of success.

When we're learning-agile, we're engaged
with the world around us. Insatiably
curious, we don't just default to the "same
old" experiences or problem solving.
We become willing to experiment—
with learning that helps inform the future.

After all, achievements fade, progress inspires,

but learning endures.

We have been here before

Amid massive change and uncertainty, there is comfort in knowing that history does repeat itself. We have faced challenges before—the Spanish Flu outbreak of 1918 and, more recently, the global financial crisis, the Great Recession, the COVID-19 pandemic.

While managing crises may not be something leaders naturally think about, it ranks in the top five of a leader's responsibilities.

So, how do we get through? By following our values and drawing from past experiences. Indeed, as the saying goes, "the more things change, the more they stay the same." Knowing that we've been here before provides context, comfort, and courage.

The effective

We've all said it occasionally—
If only I knew then
what I know now.

Think about those words
for a moment. What if in the
midst of the most troubling
circumstances we really did
"know fear"—but with the
assurance that, in the end,
things would turn out OK?
Would we ever spend so much
time worrying? Or, instead,
would we devote that time
to … [fill in the blank]?

perspective

It's an interesting perspective.
But, amid uncertainty
when ambiguity abounds,
it is hard to think that way.
Believe me, I can relate.

Earlier in my career, I left
investment banking and
joined a dot-com company
that later imploded. I spent the
next year worrying constantly.
How was I going to provide
for my five children; when
and where would I get my next
job? Then I joined Korn Ferry,
and my life changed forever.

161

If I had told myself that everything would turn out fine, what would I have done with that year? Maybe I would have learned to fly or become a scratch golfer. Who knows, I might have even taken up painting as a hobby. *Anything* would have been far more creative and productive than drowning in uncertainty.

It's the same for all of us. Time wasted on worrying is time we'll never get back.

We know we have conquered challenges before, and we will again. When we can summon that courage, we can choose how we spend the most precious of all commodities—time.

Never walk alone

I can remember being a young boy in my grandmother's house on a cold day. We had just come back from a funeral, and I was trying to get warm by standing with one foot on either side of the floor register that blew hot air from the furnace. My grandmother was singing her favorite song: "You'll Never Walk Alone." So appropriate and so timeless:

When you walk through a storm
Hold your head up high
And don't be afraid of the dark
At the end of a storm
There's a golden sky
And the sweet silver song of a lark
Walk on through the wind
Walk on through the rain
Though your dreams be tossed
and blown
Walk on, walk on
With hope in your heart
And you'll never walk alone…

Whenever something unsettling happens, our first reaction is naturally to look around at others for affirmation of how we should feel. All it takes is one person with a brave face—or someone shaking in their shoes. Human beings are social animals—we naturally look to others for connection and to create and receive assurance. When we're on our own, we are vulnerable to threats. But with others, we feel courage.

That's why the first rule in any leadership journey is never walk alone. When we travel with others, we find comfort. Together, we rise above.

Facing reality

Instead of giving up hope, it's time to take heart. We look for signs of progress—wherever and whatever they are, and no matter how small they might be. Often, making this change is merely flipping the switch of our perception. We must continually refocus our lens, as this illustration shows us.

When we look at this illustration, what do we see first? Does the vase jump out at us? Or do our eyes keep searching for the gentler, happier images of the faces of two people meeting?

Seeing only the vase locks us in the status quo—elegant yes, but without emotion or feeling. But when we gravitate toward the faces, our mindset shifts.

Give energy or take energy. Construct or criticize. It's a choice—a conscious choice. When we refocus our lens, we will indeed see our own boldness and bravery, knowing that this too shall pass.

A "peak" into our soul

While most of us will never attempt to climb the tallest mountains, we do know what it's like to feel afraid, isolated, and in danger of giving up. That's a soul-searching moment.

One of our colleagues is among only about a few hundred people on the planet to reach the "Seven Summits" of the highest peaks on every continent. On one particular climb,

she was stranded in a tent on the side of Denali, the tallest mountain in North America—withstanding temperatures of −60 degrees Fahrenheit, plus deadly windchill. Being that high up on a mountain in those conditions was like being on a different planet—totally cut off from the rest of humanity.

In that tent on Denali, she refused to give up. Instead,

she took what she had learned from previous climbs—from Denali (including failures) to Everest, where she summited on her first attempt, beating the 9-out-of-10 odds against it. She regained her courage by connecting to a sense of mission, choice, and purpose—not simply to survive, but also to thrive.

That's the power of purpose. For all of us,
purpose precedes the first step of any journey.
It is the overarching "why."

Shared purpose creates shared urgency.

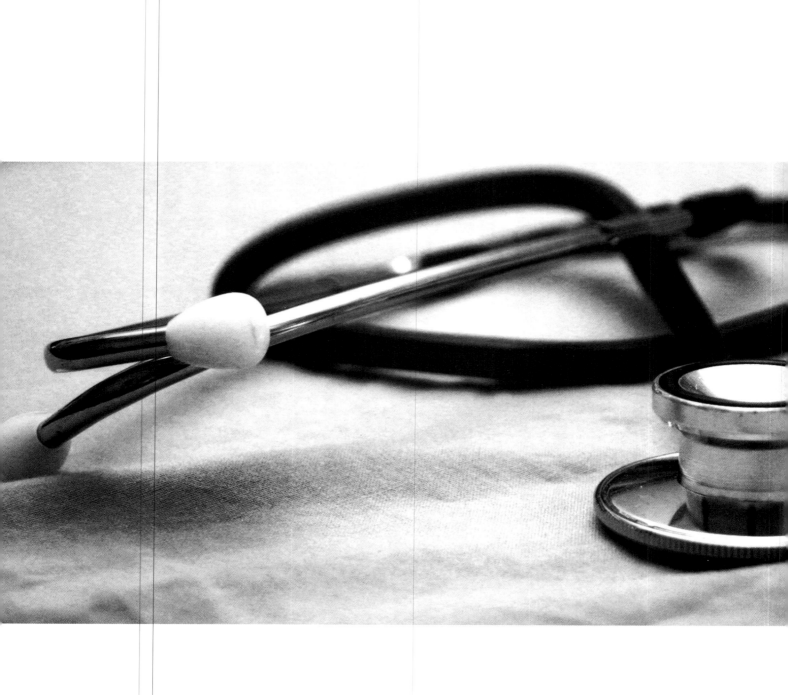

Against all odds

It's a choice we all have.

When one of my friends was only 20 years old, he was handed what felt like a death sentence. After delivering a life-altering diagnosis, a doctor told my friend that, if he took care of himself, he might live to age 45 or 50.

Rather than resigning himself to that predicted fate, my friend made the determination that he would not let this disease defeat him. He would do whatever it took to beat the odds.

Today, my friend has greatly surpassed that expectation. He has lived a life in which he has pursued everything he ever wanted to try—and continues to live life with passion.

The boldness
to be

Basketball practice was over. As the other kids waited outside the gym doors for their parents to pick them up, I started walking in the other direction—telling my teammates I had someplace else to be.

The truth, though, was that I always asked my dad to meet me a few blocks away. It was the early 1970s, and I didn't want anyone at school to see my dad's car—a 1956 Buick with a rusted bumper that belched blue clouds of exhaust.

My dad had gone bankrupt a couple of years before and we had no money. I hated going to the grocery store and always tried to pick the checkout line with the fewest people so no one would see us using food stamps.

The car, though, was just as bad for a teenager trying desperately to fit in and not stand out for the wrong reasons. As I slunk low in the seat of that old Buick, my dad knew what was going on—and I knew that he knew. But we never talked about it. He just let me be.

Today, of course, I'd love to have that old Buick to restore. Even more important, I wish I could have one more chance to open that car door and sit up tall and proud beside my dad. But that was beyond what this 13-year-old could do. I was too embarrassed and lacked the courage to know who I truly was.

No doubt almost everyone can relate. In fact, whenever I tell this story, it always amazes me how people immediately respond with their own stories. It never fails to happen. We all have our backgrounds and experiences that become the legacy we carry forward on our journey.

Being authentic is the only way to bridge the barriers—physical distance, emotional separation, and social divides. We need to boldly show who we truly are, what motivates us, and what we believe about the future.

What
gets you
moving?

It's the question we each must ask ourselves.

Are we driving to exceed our own goals?
Do we thrive when working with others and feeling
connected? Are we motivated by influencing others?

These three questions capture the essence of
three motivations—achievement, affiliation, and
power—as defined by the late David McClelland,
one of our firm's early thought leaders.

As positive drivers, they fuel discretionary
energy. Leveraging these three motivators can
help people get unstuck and moving again:

**Achievement speaks to the reality that
different work needs to get done—and
work needs to get done differently.**

**Affiliation addresses the emotional side,
with a focus on relationships that can help
people feel less isolated.**

**Power (meaning to influence) drives the
kind of change the world needs today.**

In addition to these three,
there is also a fourth motivator,
as McClelland defined later
in his work: avoidance.
It's a kind of self-protection
against unpleasant people or
circumstances. Often, avoidance
is driven by fear of rejection
or of failure. When we feel
overwhelmed, avoidance can
become our default. But that's
the opposite of what we need.

To lead others, we first have
to lead ourselves. And that
requires courage—to be humble,
to be self-aware, to honestly
look in the mirror. Then we
can mirror the behaviors
we wish to see in others.

There is always blue sky above the clouds —even on the most dismal day.

It's the leader's job to inspire others to see it.

Chapter 5
EMPATHY

Empathy is all about meeting others where they are —

to understand who they are.

I'll never forget the day. It was about two-thirty in the afternoon on a cold day with a heavy rain pouring down—and I was about 10 years old. A huge truck pulled up in front of our house; its back doors swung open, and the ramp was brought down.

As two men approached our house, I looked past them to the truck and wondered, were we moving? When my dad came up beside me, there were tears in his eyes. "Son, it will be OK," he said. Then I watched as those men carried our furniture out the front door. My father had gone bankrupt, and everything was being repossessed.

Almost everyone has these kinds of stories—often the "stories behind the stories" —of hardships and losses. These are the experiences that strengthen our work ethic, shape our values, and make us stronger.

These pivotal moments carry other lessons as well. They teach us compassion and empathy.

185

The E in

Empathy is the "E" in grace.
This last letter completes
grace's many meanings, from
gratitude and resilience through
aspiration and courage, and
now empathy, which allows us
to meet others where they are.

Empathy is the catalyst that
turns "we're all in this together"
from only words to a feeling
and then to an action.

Grace

It broadcasts, verbally and nonverbally,

" I know how you feel. Our circumstances may be different, but I've been there, too. *"*

People are not all
the same—nor are they
in the same place.

It takes empathy—the cornerstone of radically human leadership—to connect genuinely with others as we journey together, leaving the familiar for the unknown.

The empathic brain

Empathy is composed of three slightly different but crucial components—each providing nuance to this complex emotion. By using brain imaging, we can literally see how each aspect of empathy engages our minds and emotions.

The first is **cognitive empathy,** which allows us to understand others' emotional experiences while maintaining a healthy detachment. This is how we intellectually walk in someone else's shoes.

The second is **sympathy**—also known as emotional empathy. This allows us to feel what another person is experiencing. While it has value, there are limitations—as brain imaging reveals. Sympathy activates brain circuits in a way that makes the observer feel pain as if it were their own. When suffering becomes too intense, we are prone to protect ourselves by putting up barriers, thus reducing the likelihood that we will act with compassion.

The third is **compassion**, or empathetic care, which we experience as concern for others. This form of empathy activates a set of brain regions involved in feelings of warmth, reward, and affiliation. In fact, highly compassionate people are able to quiet the parts of their brain that focus on themselves so they can help others.

Leaders must pay attention to the nuances of empathy and work to develop interpersonal skills across all three dimensions. That way, their empathy will not only be seen and felt by others, it will also be on target in its effectiveness.

The times, they are a'changin'

Bob Dylan said it best: "The times they are a-changin'"—and so are the conversations. More real, more emotional, often happening for the first time. And that's a good thing.

Communication today must be authentic. It looks at reality unblinkingly and forms a bridge, heart to heart.

In the past, leaders were seen more as a function than as people. Those days have been fading fast as leaders' roles require more of them.

As leaders, we need to show more of who we are as people—as someone who is empathetic and trustworthy. It's a reflection of what has been happening everywhere, as people are leading with their hearts and seeking to understand.

Leadership is always about transporting others from one place to another, including emotionally. It takes communication—honest and heartfelt—to truly understand others and their emotions. Communication is where leadership lives and breathes.

Through the
lens of others

Empathy rules the day—meeting others where they are, understanding their experiences. It changes everything, including how we interact.

We used to say, "How are you?"; now it's "how are you feeling?" But that's not all. The more empathetic we are, the more we broaden our view. We see beyond our own perspective—through the lens of others.

After all, what we do is not

who we are.

The language of inclusion

The secret of success on the leadership journey is fostering a culture of inclusion. To create that environment, we need to speak the language—then walk the talk.

Diversity is a fact. Differences make each person unique.

Inclusion, however, is a behavior. Inclusion values and fully leverages different perspectives and backgrounds to drive results.

Engagement is an emotion. The emotional connection leaders have with their team determines the collective level of discretionary energy.

Leaders who are fluent in the language and action of inclusion become culturally agile. They fully embrace and leverage the vast diversity of today's workforces. When this happens, empowerment becomes purposeful power.

When an organization is truly inclusive, everyone's perspective and input matters. People know it's safe to speak "their truth." Conflict about what people perceive isn't discouraged—that's how collective genius is born.

People are empowered to ask not just why, but also why not—to think not only in probability, but also in possibility. This requires more than just encouraging a behavior—it must be a cultural muscle that gets exercised

How inclusive are you?

Identifying biases and promoting conscious inclusion may at times be uncomfortable, but those efforts must be sustained. For example, leaders need to communicate why it's important to go beyond diversity alone to reach "conscious inclusion" —where curiosity about differences is encouraged and where inclusion is the mutual responsibility of all people.

Challenging? Yes. Emotional? Very.

The first step is to increase self-awareness around inclusion by asking ourselves the following questions:

How does your unconscious bias influence your behavior?

When making decisions, how often do you take the initiative to seek out different viewpoints?

Do you catch yourself in moments when you make assumptions about others?

Do you actively listen in all conversations, no matter who is speaking?

In times of change, do you show greater interest in your difficulty or the difficulties of others?

An unforgettable

lesson

I searched and searched
for the dusty field in the
small town in Kansas where
I spent some of my childhood.
Later, I saw that it was gone.

Yet that place remained
etched in my mind—looming
large in my memory as the
setting of where I learned
a powerful lesson.

I was in fourth grade, and
we were playing kickball.
But on one particular day,
the coach changed the rules.
He randomly called people
out when they were clearly
safe and also called them safe
when they were clearly out.

When he did it with me,
my competitiveness got the
best of me. "Why do you
keep doing that?" I asked.

The coach paused and
waited patiently until I was
listening. "Now you have
a taste of what so many
people live with every day."

That had been his intent,
as coach and teacher, all along—
to give us a wider perspective;
not telling us what to think,
but rather what to think about.

I never forgot that experience—
my first taste of the importance
of inclusive leadership.

Inclusion fuels passion.
When people feel seen
and heard it becomes a
powerful intrinsic motivator.
It taps people's deep-seated
desire to know that they
belong, make a difference,
and are part of something
bigger than themselves.
Motivated by purpose
and energized by passion,
they are more likely to
commit to the journey.

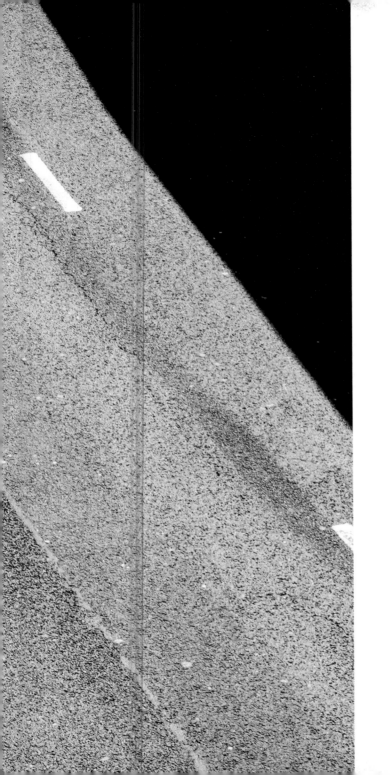

Inclusive leadership
converts self-interest
into shared interest.

Today's

A small or even insignificant event can create
a much bigger impact—like the proverbial butterfly
flapping its wings that stirs the wind into a tornado.

Leaders can leverage the butterfly effect as subtle
shifts take hold and then ripple through their
organizations, creating significant changes in how
people think, act, and connect with each other—
with greater empathy and understanding.

The leader's job is to shine a spotlight on those
small and sometimes barely perceptible shifts
—to see the butterfly within the caterpillars that
can't yet get off the ground, but sincerely want to try.

**Indeed, there is
a leader within
each of us.**

butterfly effect

It's how things get done

Ask six people to define culture, and you'll probably get 12 different answers. Some say it's the mission and the values; for others, it's ping-pong tables and work attire.

Culture, though, boils down to just one definition—it's how things get done. When empathy is part of the fabric of culture, it permeates not only what we do, but also why.

When I was growing up, the minute I walked into my aunt's house, I had to kick off my sneakers at the door. The reason? The pride of this Midwest household was a white shag carpet, and my aunt kept it spotless. There were clear plastic runners across the rug to walk on, which matched the plastic coverings on the furniture.

Best of all—they raked the carpet with a special rake to make it look like new.

I didn't have to do any of these things at home—but their house, their rules. When I got a little older, though, it occurred to me why these things were so important. My aunt and uncle didn't have a lot of money, and they worked hard for anything they had—she as a nurse, and he at an oil refinery.

By seeing their rules in this light, I came to appreciate even more their work ethic and values. That was the culture that made their house a home.

We're all deciding on "house rules" these days—the *why* as well as the *where* of how work gets done. But just like the carpet rake and the plastic runners, we can't get caught up in the form—the protocols and procedures. Far more important is the substance—how people actually engage and interact with each other. We won't find it spelled out in some handbook. It's not captured in some slogan on a website or a poster in the hallway.

Culture can be a bit of a conundrum. I can remember a client meeting a few years ago, when every member of their senior team was asked to define their culture. As each person spoke, it became clear that they were focused only on the form—not the substance. But when the question changed—"What is it like to be an employee here?"—the answers were from the heart, stripped of jargon, and laser-focused on how work gets done.

The language of culture is emotion—the spirit of how we do things. Culture is a celebration of what we hold as important—what we believe and hold sacred. And it's up to the leader to take it from invisible *to visible.*

Cultivating

culture

When it comes to the care and feeding of culture, the leader plays a disproportionately large role. Indeed, culture starts at the top. That's where a culture of empathy and inclusion is created and shaped.

Leaders have two distinct core roles. First, they are the culture champions—the role models who embody the mindset, beliefs, and desired behaviors. Second, they are the culture architects— who make sure that the right structures are in place to support those desired behaviors.

By word and example, leaders ensure that a healthy, inclusive culture takes root and grows. But it takes time. After all, merely shouting louder at a plant won't make it grow faster. It takes the right conditions for cultivation.

The Me-O-Meter

It's a simple gauge that anyone can use to assess just how empathetic they are, especially as leaders. When we speak, are we more likely to use "I," "me," and "my"? Or do we always speak about "we," "us," and "our"?

The Me-O-Meter can really open our eyes!

Enlightened leaders speak from "we" and do so almost exclusively, especially when talking about goals and accomplishments. The only exception is when leaders are making tough decisions and must willingly accept the consequences of those decisions.

Listening to others with the Me-O-Meter in mind can really make an impact. Like when I interviewed a person who told me, "I recruited 40 people over the past year." Really? Somehow, I doubt that was a single-handed endeavor. The far more accurate and impactful thing to say would have been, "Our team recruited 40 people over the past year."

It's a powerful reminder: Leaders don't accomplish anything by themselves.

After all, it's the players who win games.

It's all
about
others

When leaders talk, is anyone really listening? The best way to ensure that the audience is tuned in is to emotionalize and personalize communication—who we are, what we believe, what we value, and what matters most. The leader, as the steward of the organization's narrative, must ensure that authentic, relatable themes are woven into the messages they communicate.

What matters most is not what the leader says, but what others hear. They need to know that they are seen—first for who they are, and then for what they do.

It starts with us.

Awareness awakens. To lead others, we must first lead ourselves. Before we do anything else, we take a look in the mirror at our values, motivations, strengths, and blind spots. By knowing ourselves we can manage ourselves first. Then we will be better able to truly see and understand others—and positively impact them.

But it's not about us. We're not sculptors working alone in a studio, chipping marble or molding clay. We aren't solo performers. We work with and through others, with greater empathy and deeper appreciation.

Quite simply, our success
is always measured in
what others achieve.

Acknowledgments

I met Dan Gugler early in my career as CEO of Korn Ferry. When we first met I told him that I wanted to share Korn Ferry's voice on leadership. I have learned over and again as CEO that you can never accomplish anything on your own—our success comes from the power of working with others. Dan has guided me to better understand that, and he has continuously enabled me to expand the lessons that I have learned from working with others.

Over a decade ago I was having lunch with a colleague, and we were talking about the unique ability some people have to share their observations and feelings, in words, with others. She looked at me and said, "You have to talk with Tricia Crisafulli." Trusting that recommendation, I called up our team in Los Angeles, and we got to work. It didn't take long to see how Tricia, already an accomplished author, was able to help our firm. Before we knew it, she was traveling around the world on our behalf, interviewing leaders from every industry.

None of our learning and discussion would have been possible without the collective gratitude, resilience, aspiration, courage, and empathy of the thousands of people who are part of the Korn Ferry family. Our family includes diverse personalities who possess incredible talents—from generations past, some with shorter visits, and many long-tenured friends.

I extend my most profound thank you to Dan, Tricia, and the countless others across our company who have helped me learn the grace of leadership.

I'd also like to thank our extremely talented Korn Ferry Lab team, including Jonathan Pink, Hayley Kennell, Maria Kalavrezou, and others for designing this book. They have a magical ability to seamlessly put concepts into design—and the result is nothing less than art. And thanks as always to Brian Neill and the team at Wiley, our publishing partner, for helping us on the journey.